Water Street

ACKNOWLEDGMENTS

Grateful acknowledgement is given to the editors of these journals, in which
poems in this chapbook first appeared:

The Cape Rock—"Tractatus"
The Naugatuck River Review—"Frogs"
Pirene's Fountain—"Lines from Base Camp"
Silkworm—"Elegy"

Publisher: Leah Maines

Editor: Christen Kincaid

Cover Art: Stephen Petegorsky Photography

Author Photo: Jermane Stephinger

Cover Design: Elizabeth Maines McCleavy

Printed in the USA on acid-free paper.
Order online: www.finishinglinepress.com
also available on amazon.com

Author inquiries and mail orders:
Finishing Line Press
P. O. Box 1626
Georgetown, Kentucky 40324
U. S. A.

Water Street

poems by

Naila Moreira

Finishing Line Press
Georgetown, Kentucky

Table of Contents

Water Street

A fragrance fills the garden,
making me forget everything.
It smells like oleander and pollen.
It smells like the asphodel.
Like Circe's garden.

To live here I left my husband,
I left the world.
The scent floats over the waterfall
that endlessly washes the earth clean.
My brothers are wasps and spiders,
the mink that lives under the stones.
Shapeshifter, weaver,
master of two realms.

Here, I have no children,
only poems.

Tractatus

We cannot describe the limits of language
Or point them out to someone. Thus wrote Wittgenstein
In the *Tractatus Logico-Philosophicus*, I don't know what page, since
I only read the Cliff Notes,
Having really had Tractatus in bed last night beside me
Opposite the blond-headed half-awake bloke at my left thigh.
He, perhaps, would have heard beyond my phrases,
Had the reality of my body, where I lay between possibilities,
Poked on two sides, the corners of Tractatus being also very hard,
Not been so distracting;
Instead he thought my meanings ordinary enough and quite
    manageable,
Coming, as they seemed to him, one after the other
Instead of outlining in fluorescent starlight of stick-on constellations
Circles into infinity and past him
As I had first intended.

Insomnia

A satellite
Circles my house tonight
White dust

And I am thrown
Into a dream

Where the sky gets bigger and bigger
Choked by stars
That grow like pinwheels

Their centers
Mad, circling eyes.

The soul floats above sleep
Like a boat over a lake.
Come, ferryman.

Let us journey the world tonight,
Lamps on a surface

Rinsed of daylight.
The heart is a dark water
That shines.

Wife

Over the tomatoes, the onions,
The day is blueing beyond.
High summer. Cottony particles
Drift through the evening, past
The motionless curtains,
Past the stove. This ignites;
A knife bites, the air fills with acid,
Protesting entry to the layers of the world.
O, pearl. O bursting tomato,
O the salt cod in layers beneath,
Cold ocean journeyer, cleaned and caught
In the Pyrex dish, on the kitchen counter,
Breathing sea under the soil
Of taut skinned root, of bright fruit.
Within, a hidden shame
To be chopping inside these walls,
Not to unskin myself, and join
The bare world, earth's production.
Veils fall beyond the window,
Trickling over my sight.
The body of earth is so easy to imagine,
So difficult to touch.
O melding of flavors in the pan,
O layers like the planet itself,
O food for a continent or merely a husband,
The closest one can get to desire.

Grass

We tend to rely on it.
Trusting the peace
Of a green and fertile home
We build our gardens of it.
The unity
Of a calm and prosperous country
Is in its single-mindedness.
Growing straight
Like swords, like needles,
It knits together a nation
And destroys the earth.

Ode on *The Scream*

The Scream is a painting by Edvard Munch.

Because life is a living madness;
Because blue, not black, is the color of death;
Because the world will end in fire;
Because the magician requires the absurd;
Because the absurd is a dangerous portal;
Because silence is the most powerful protest;
Because yellow and red are my favorite color;
Because the Yellow House was insanity's color;
Because the ear is a dangerous portal;
Because a poem is a paintbrush;
Because no one in fact can speak out loud;
Because passers-by cannot see or hear;
Because the bridge doesn't span the river;
Because the river can't reach the bridge;
Because turning liquid is the madman's greatest dream;
Because we cannot sing with whales
Or repeat the water's endless conversation;
Because drownings and ovens are fates for witches;
Because ovens are the 20th century's avatar;
Because an oven is a choice and a doom;
Because the ash turns the sky red;
Because of the combustion engine;
Because the world is melting away;
Because a Norwegian in a crushed continent;
Because of two world wars and blood;
Because war is sponsored suicide;
Because a gun is a dangerous portal;
Because a paintbrush is a gun.

Sickness

Fighting the yellow fight
In a dream, I crouch by the window.
This is my blue body,
The shade of my eyelid over the world.

Caught behind this square,
Retching, I am patient through
Exhaustion's resignation.
Sickness has absorbed me,

I am no longer an eye.
Here in this hot physique,
This pulsing interior,
I find the blood of my blood,

The skin in my skin,
The stomach within my stomach.
An airplane screams
Beyond, and I hardly know it.

It takes the delicate damp
Of a sudden rain to reach me.
A sheeted symphony, invisible,
Silently mists the soul.

Living Room

The night is black
and no words stir.

The radiator
roars, like hell's fire.

A heart strives
against its bands of steel,

Achillean fool,
stubborn to its doom.

The refrigerator,
unpoetic word,

chokes its compressor
into its double self,

frozen as an Arctic,
belching heat behind.

So we live,
hearts on ice

minds and hands a furnace,
shoveling coal.

The world burns.
Rows of bodies

sleep on the sidewalk.
No room at the inn,

they're burning Bethlehem.

*

Clouds of snowflakes,
each one a bird.

The fields sapped
of their milkweed,

sepia now.
Old photos of the past,

these too were green
and full of secrets.

Now all is bare.
The hunter floats

over dead grasses.

*

Don't let history
eat me whole.

I too am a rocket:
rocket girl,

lost to earth.
Far above this room,

this dry cell,
its membrane as inexorable

as life,
my thoughts explode

into stars.
The corner television coughs and murmurs,

loathe to let me go.

Mt. Tom

Hiking—the day grey, leading
Autumn leaves to glow
With a strange light—

Your footsteps chased my own,
The day too warm
For such a late date.

We found a hickory nut,
Hard, promising in the pocket.
We took it home.

Cracked by a well-placed blow
It unveiled its secret.
A white maggot, curled in the heart.

The meat had turned
To powder, inedible, only
Black, papery membranes left behind.

Cloudy spots of quartz
Shine from within dull stone,
Glaucous eyes, unseeing;

A cataract, history of water
Injected into veins,
Vapor puddled and exhaled.

The bedrock is a body,
Aged, riddled with doubt
And thought.

The earth has caught my sickness.

To Leonard Cohen

Reading you
Warms me
From the upper thigh
To the navel.
Is that not strange?
You speak of loose philosophy,
Of a shack by a river,
Of the small melodrama
Endlessly unconsummated,
The labor pains
Of a baby that will not be born,
The child of your art,
The link of your loins
To a woman who must always
Be too far away to absorb.
I too am too far
For you to love me,
As you have loved all women:
With the sadness of respect
And condescension,
The unutterably distant touch.

Loreley

I drop like a stone into the task you have given:
It closes on me like a mouth,
The silvery mouth of the water, reflecting
All you expect of me.

Down here fishes grub like plows:
Grim weeds, algae-fronded,
Are the sole harvest of their flap-lipped gums.
The ancient silts lift to surround me.

Meanwhile I lie heavy, hair afloat
Like reeds reaching toward a strange warped sky.
The sunlight bends like straws.
And you'll come splashing through before too long,

Haul me up by my locks, thinking me pretty
Painted as I am by mirroring swells;
And from my throat I'll spit the muddy vowels
Sedimented by the hours.

Frogs

Last night the frogs died under my wheels;
I killed them, at three a.m. in a downpour.
From some dark knothole, invented from nowhere,
Sacrificial, with a death-wish,
They seemed to leap under the car.
But it was my fault I killed them,
Angry, driving late
And fast, whipping down the country roads
Instead of the highway
Because they were beautiful
And dark, and far.
I cried as I hit them
And slowed the car to a crawl,
Trying to see them first, but still they rose,
Unexpected, small white innocent forms
Like phantom children jumping in the rain.
They were, perhaps, trying
To make more of themselves,
Away from the eye of man:
The hundred, the thousand, slick ghost shapes from the marshes
That one road splits.
Why couldn't I leave them alone?

The Golden Turtle Faces the World

The rim of the shell shone a tantalizing copper
As if its substance had transmuted
Overnight, unasked, a galvanic new dawn.

Inside, still the same vault, gleaming
Dully the color of old treasures.
This cave of the dragon, inscribed

With soldered linkages of plates,
A tectonic array, pure logic of the hexagon,
Familiar order, a continent of self.

Just past, a world waiting, no detail.
White sky, a possibility of sun.
Electricity of hope and fear, an opening.

He stared. His eyes, a mess of folds and water,
His hands, rough despite soft living,
Claws shining with guard, catching the light.

A nut uncracked. Inviolate nugget at lake's bottom.
A hundred secrets safe. Thirty years of waiting.
The fussed limnology of professors,

Delicate bell jars of the daphnia.
A fine dust of time, leavings of patient rivers
Settling on his skin, the only intruder.

But they had called. He could hear from above
The bell-like summons.
A sacrifice—a ritual celebration—

Would he be prophet, would he be sacred—
Mutilated, would he be fed to the dogs,
His shell taken?

Finding even gold tarnished, verdigris of fear.
Growth's green patina, flawlessness a lie,
Taken prisoner in unleashing him.

He stirred. An explosion of mud
Rose from layered glacial past. All was now to be
Offered, a monster, a mouthpiece,

The alchemy of fools or of the wisest,
A shattering light, a column of water,
Channel to the ordinary, to transcendence.

Late Berries

1. Doubt

A thousand crab apples
Sparkling red across the blue sky.
Thick Concord grapes, dripping
Purple from a fence of sandalwood yellow.
A small frog rescued
From the road, turned loose at the edge of the swamp.
Everything fertile, even the mud
Gummed with promise for next year.
Who am I, then, who am I,
Who am I to question meaning in this world?
To rise at four, empty,
And stare into the blank gray face of dawn,
Seeing nothing, the robins' song gone
Into harvest season, nestlings flown?
Their high journeys soon will start,
Pole to pole, senseless and invincible,
Great arcs, like the travelings of the stars.

2. Endurance

It's five pm, and still
There is sunlight on the water.
No one needs anything from me
But that I sit here, reading poems.
For sure, winter is coming.
Soon the light will go earlier
Behind the dark pines on the hill.
But for now I am quiet and warmed.
A robber fly on sunned granite
Rests from his stealing of lives.
Words, like small gnats, hum

In this moment before the decline.
I am on the last page of my notebook.
I am on the last page of my notebook—
But behind me the sepia flowers
Of the year's last hydrangeas
Imprint air with their drying sachets:
These fragrant old photos,
White sprays of mesh lace,
My mother's face, that will always be mine.

3. Maenads

The goldenrod, the pokeweed berries
Dripping in late heat; autumn
Splashing sun about, as from a tipped
Bucket of summer's paint. Stolen hues
Deepen with the touch of her hand's love:
An artist grand at theft, transforming each
To something new. Her laughter
Is no mothering sound; she is a maenad,
Inconstant, here today, tomorrow gone,
But the casual press of her dry palm
On the sweating sickness of the modern
Brow, tempts with illusions of her gifts,
Her love, her safety, harvest, fertile womb
That bears—then kills its children in our sight.
Should I stay? Her dryad flippancy
Is power, is freedom, hope. Her easel drips
With careless blows of paint. She is the master.
Her paintbrush is her sword, and when she falls
On it, hues fading brown, life bleeding out,
It is the memory of her stays our hand
From following; the stores of her we kept.

Lines from Base Camp

The silence reminds
that aloneness is all there is—
that on the edge of a great crag
we stand waiting,
a cliff behind us
and a chasm before us,
wide space beside us
and black night above us,
and that within the self,
as dark as the great depths,
it is there we create the beloved

The Bat

How small it was—
Crawling across the gravel drive, a mouse
With arms grotesquely fanned, a faint

Dark angel. How God must make his creatures
Suffer, cry of pain as the wings are fashioned,
Reaching from inside the soul to drag

Material into a sail; crafting
The strut that stays the gauze. On these
They eat the wind, its small denizens,

Wings consuming wings. Strange fate.
But this one plied no air, carried no
Whisk of flight, churned no summer

To froth. This one, eyes half shut, struggled
A way across a desert of stone,
Precinct of its flightless brethren. And I,

Halting my bicycle just in time,
Bent to stare at its efforts, high dignity
Dropped. Stumbling pain and defeat. I ran

Inside, to grab a dishtowel, homely
Haven, returned to gather it up:
Weakly its curved claws grabbed,

Hooks grappling to climb a mountain.
The wedge-head bobbled. Could this, I wondered,
Frail being be made ordinary, even

Fallen and ugly, like this? Not built
For the world of the ground, it looked
Malformed. Freakish. Wrong. I laid

My gargoyle on a stone windowsill,
By a bush I thought would protect it. But no:
It scrambled from there, and almost fell,

Barely clinging, by one long toe,
Quavering, black smear on granite.
Its world was upside down.

So gently I ushered it up once again.
Brought it into the shed. Old rakes,
Clay pots, shovels, garden gloves,

Leading to a lightless cave. Back here,
On one rafter, wooden door cracked open,
Letting in just one splice of sun,

I placed my bundle, watched it squirm
And crawl like a baby. Here, I thought, safety.
It almost tumbled. But reaching back

To the dawn of batness, its most deep
Atavistic self, the prehistoric
Hand-feet snatched, and held to wood,

To cloth, and it dangled, as bats should.
How thin it was! Mere suggestion of bat,
Shade even of those shades that fill

The air with black veils. Cousins of mystery,
Borderlands' children, enablers of witches,
Villagers of the dark. Rags from a burst

Of dead leaves again living.
But this one just looked like a mouse.
Small faced, pinched, it faced the day's flash

With compressed anguish. Eyes clamped shut.
I watched its small breathing. Its chest rebounding.
Survive, I willed it. Remain, small beast,

Window of night, errant shred of flight,
Sky's platypus. Prophet of dusk
For those that can hear: the highest of songs.

I left it there sleeping, its rapid heart beating,
Filling the shed with its pulse.
Then I had to go out to the world:

By the time I returned, it had died.

The population of North American bats has declined by 80% since white-nosed fungal disease emerged in 2007.

Modern Song

I would like a cat to hold.
I would like to be in Argentina.
I would like to sleep to the sound of the river.
I would like to be taken to dinner in the city—
or in an old mill building converted to a fine restaurant.

I would like to be somewhere outside of time.
I would like to be with you.
I would like to breathe salt air from a high balcony.
I would like to hear whippoorwills calling—
their high strange whoops in the sweet, fragrance-heavy southern air.

I would like to be eighteen and foolish.
I would like to believe in ideals.
I would like to feel the winds of a high plateau—
see great flocks of migratory birds settling, air crackling with their cries.

I would like to melt like mercury.
I would like to burn like a flare.
I would like to be everything, everything
that draws the eye,
that thrums the ear,
that incinerates.

Injured at Field Camp

I lay on the warm bunk by the door,
Sun spilling in from the Montana afternoon.
Half of me slept. Half of me was aware
Of the kitten stretched out along my sternum.
He was cloud-grey, son of the cat
Whose needle-clawed offspring, fuzzy, bold,
Tumbled in the roadside dust by the hedge.
I followed them on my rickety
Crutches, slow, awkward, good for nothing,
While my peers worked, mapping the mountains.
High in the peaks they worked, fighting
Up and down the slopes, up and down,
Surmounting this summit, winning this valley,
Muscles set to another mountain.
I had left their ranks. I waited alone in the still
Of heat and afternoon. Just past camp the creek bubbling.
At noon the dining staff made me small lunch
And I sifted away with it.
The insects' pace was mine, the pace of snails,
If snails could've lived in this dry landscape.
Out in the pastures must have been ranchers and cows;
Here, in the barracks, only me.

See how the clouds dwarf the mountains,
Said my friend, a wise young man
As he sat chewing a grass blade on the cliff's edge.
Clouds pillared tall in the impassive sky,
Unforgiving, rainless. Now I lay in dry air,
Softly dry as a kitten, around my face,
While the real kitten once again stretched its bright claws,
Made a small whining exhale, and once more slept.
How peaceful it was to say no to it all
Save the kitten, and rest. My displaced hip
Lay like the broken shapes of a doll

That has been badly used, in a child's hospital;
The strength of my body, so often relied on,
Long muscles, perfect, sinewy, lean,
All useless; and lassitude spread like the heat,
Like the sun, whose fingers touched me past the door.
The crutches leaned, unburnt matchsticks of time,
Against the bunk. The world was silent,
While kitten-furred eloquence rose from the depths
And blessed me.

Winter Field

Who am I—the frozen winter field,
austere, aloof, fills the outward view,
cheeks raw with wind, the thrill
of the utterly alien landscape and alien soul

of silence. Small flocks of birds
blow past as if there's nothing for them here,
even though all their small lives' fuel
hides in tiny grains lost between the stalks

that rattle as my mind rattles, correspondence
between me and this emptied field, its core
plush with meat for the merlin, though the vista
lies blank, with seemingly nothing to say—

restless space, night winds will rock
across your wastes like a tambourine.
The emerging stars an emptiness
over an emptiness, a flight of sparrows.

2015

The first meteors of the year are set to peak
Tonight. Fireballs, flashes
Promise to explode the sweet
Face of darkness. But, predictors say,
Full moon will blind the watchers, if the clouds
Don't eat the fireshow first. The brain
Rebels against necessity in the world
And vows to keep awake this evening anyway:
Let flatness take the earth's whole face—
Still stars will pierce the ceiling of the mind.

Down here, planes fall, frogs spawn
Against backdrop of rubber, plastic, steel;
A thousand eggs; a thousand tiny bombs.
They hatch into a universe of fear.
Their planetary destiny is clear:
To die, if not tomorrow, then today.
Like lamps they fill the waters, atoms
Round and pitted with a nuclear eye,
Transforming into embryos, they writhe
And shock: life, interruptive and surreal.

All things on earth are round, the poet said,
Circling to their core. Then why this arm,
This leg? Flat surfaces proliferate
In cities: buildings, towers, airfields, roads,
But fronds still vanquish geometric shapes
In time. The planets fall from endless height
To pockmark the cold sea. Stone buried in anemones.
Their mouths engulf the waters, innocence
As ravenous as war, as sin, as charm.
No drop exists on earth that has not passed
Through the twisted gut of one of these.

Life is surprise. What's real can't be defined
Nor proven. First the actual, then words.
This mouth, this flower, this monster, tentacled,
Is just a game of language, 'til the hand
Sticks to grip of nematocysts; the bright
Red and green are nothing to the thought
Until the eye contains them. In the sky
Bursting with meteors, our faith descries
Its own justification. Undescribed,
Living things still grow on undeterred.

The ponderous sky, the aching sea. The most
Insubstantial thing of all, the air
Burns with greater power under the stars.
Meteors blaze a path through it, the lost
Birds of autumn churn it, and the frost
Falls from it, too heavy to be held.
And yet it holds primeval power of breath,
Mediator between life and death,
And, by rumpled arms of ocean cradled,
Lord over even that vast indifference.

This is the vast exhale, vapor laden,
Molecularly present in the world,
That meters swash of wave and gust of storm.
This inhale gathers in all that we feed it,
Sweeps back on us, more weighty than before—
Sweet like a transplanted lung, but sick
As the body that the other's been torn from;
Its wheeze among the cliffs a serenade
Of a lost earth of which it cannot speak.
Its intercourse with earth births an unknown
Soul into our mouths. One full of threat.

For everything has changed. The synapses
Of the metropolis by night a brain
Each pulse of which reflects a human pain,
Striving to know, to build, to gain, to be.
Towers fume like cigarettes. Light climbs
Upward into a heartless cosmos. Cold
Steel reflects to steely supernovas,
Glow meets glow high in the rarified
Stratosphere. Photographer in helicopter door
Meets the prospects of that icy height,

Looks down upon the neurons of our span,
Information burning through the streets,
The anthill of our efforts. Greater than
The single human mind, this consciousness—
Or is it? Still the poet is just one
Atom in this whirling breath of action,
But must assert a place. The juggernaut
Of future set relentlessly in motion
Will gust her to an unplanned destiny,
But amid reckless coopting of her thought
By automatism, yet she has to think it.

Still there is also calm, here.
Between skyscrapers, gulls lift on the wind,
White like falling feathers, like the pure
Face of the absolved. Dissolved brine
Disinfects the city of its stenches.
No filth can persist long against nature.
All will be scrubbed, converted, modernized
By being made primitive. Cold shore, young birches,
Polypores, slime mold, mushrooms, colors
Repossess the gray of sidewalk cracks,
Reasserting everything the frozen city lacks.

After all, the woods' green scent is mold:
Soil-damp mycelia spreading, net
Of being and of killing, of eating and of rot.
Stars spangle this torn forest sod,
White constellations built of what is not.
Leaves are reborn to leaves, the trunks
Form ancient as the earth. Below the cold
January blanket, insects sleep.
Only these fungi act; a deep
Heart of frost turns over. Secrets.

These too will be memorialized in stone.
Layer upon layer accumulates,
Persistent doppelganger of decay.
Alive, they call the earth, in its own way:
In its remaking every ounce as stubborn.
The mountains: a millennial hourglass.
The soil and sand: a parchment of the past.
Fortune-teller earth; horizons darken,
Record of the ever-changing sky,
Dictating now our living history.

So one stands here, in the dark, in the chill.
Snow gathers on the lashes—stars,
Bounded by clouds, molecules, cars.
Headlights shatter the perfect still
Of solitude. A human meteor.
Tornados of blown snow lift from the street,
And the heart coils in, resisting, seeking its core.
To fuse with the world's bedlam of respiration,
To make the strained air into life or a poem,
That's what makes it worth standing out here for.

Elegy

for Bob Lipton

How the peepers cry in the forest,
How they cry, as the maples burst with flower
And my heart cries for the lost ones.
The voices lift in the dark, to the rough
Concrete of where I stand now.
You too were once young, you who abandoned
Your journey in the spring of the year
And left us to the heart of the greater darkness
That surrounds us, always.
Like wild hounds on a hunt, the frogs, like wild
Carillons from the dawn of the world;
Chasing down the prey of life, of re-creation,
Spawning; and then dying.

Traveling the Connecticut

It moves, dark silver in the half-light of dawn.
Restless traveler, what a multitude you carry:
Whole islands dissolved in the glitter of your smile.
You are not more than your burdens.
In the melting light, it sweetens the land
With a breath of gentle rot, a cloud of gnats.
Inside the mechanics of this imitation,
The train windows trembling, we marry its path
For a time. Two swans on the pewter
Shine, like the impossible thing we keep making, over and over.

Portal

"You have the key,
The little lamp spreads a ring on the stair,
Mount."   -T.S. Eliot

Here is the number on the door,
In lobby dark with promise or dismay.
Down the back steps, above the ratted rug,
Open, I say:
To tunnel of white walls and wooden floor.
Spread out, like muted hue of early dawn
The broadness of a room above the street
Where refuse of a life has strayed beyond
The tables that it ought to have stayed on:
The clothing and the dishes splashed about.
Here, the plight
Of substantive betrays ethereal,
Yet smeared with buttered sun between the leaves
Retains a certain magic in despite.
A door buried in darkness in the hill.
Room opening to windows on the trees.
The street thrums with its usual human bees.
Open to me:
This thickly lived neglect, this space apart.
The plants potted in rich earth on the sill,
This beating heart.

Letters

My friend, I send you these letters from the mountain.
Today the mountainsides are limpid in light.
The morning is sweet. The magnolias are fragrant.
When I went to rip out a sheet to send you a missive,
A voice spoke to me out of the clean
Table, out of the counter, the washed white walls,
The wicker basket of fruit,
The small carved ornaments above the stove.
Be careful, it said, when you tear out pages.
Be sure you know which book you're tearing from,
For the book of desire has petals
Close-pressed as the tightest rose,
And when they burst from the bud none can stop them
From flowering.

Naila Moreira was born in London to Brazilian parents, and grew up in New Hampshire. She studied at Amherst College and earned her doctorate at the University of Michigan. After continuing west to Seattle, working *en route* as a journalist and environmental consultant, she returned to her native New England. She now teaches at Smith College with a focus on science and nature writing.

Her science journalism has appeared in Boston Globe, Seattle Times, Science News, and the Detroit Free Press, and she writes a monthly environment column for the *Daily Hampshire Gazette*. Her poems and nature essays have been published in *The Cape Rock, The Naugatuck River Review, Pirene's Fountain, Silkworm, The Common Online*, and other literary journals. Her first chapbook, *Gorgeous Infidelities*, was published in 2014 by Impossible Dream Editions as an art book in collaboration with internationally recognized photographer Paul Ickovic. She is currently writer in residence at the Forbes Library in Northampton, Massachusetts for 2015-2018.

CPSIA information can be obtained
at www.ICGtesting.com
Printed in the USA
LVOW10s0342280417
532486LV00013B/106/P